THE
Mission of Theology
AND
Theology as Mission

Christian Mission and Modern Culture

EDITED BY
ALAN NEELY, H. WAYNE PIPKIN,
AND WILBERT R. SHENK

In the series:

Believing in the Future, by David J. Bosch

Write the Vision, by Wilbert R. Shenk

Truth and Authority in Modernity,
by Lesslie Newbigin

Religion and the Variety of Culture,
by Lamin Sanneh

The End of Christendom and the Future of Christianity,
by Douglas John Hall

The Mission of Theology and Theology as Mission,
by J. Andrew Kirk

THE

Mission of Theology

AND

Theology as Mission

J. ANDREW KIRK

TRINITY PRESS INTERNATIONAL
Valley Forge, Pennsylvania

Gracewing.

First published by
TRINITY PRESS INTERNATIONAL
P.O. Box 851
Valley Forge, PA 19482–0851
U.S.A.

First British edition
published by
GRACEWING
2 Southern Avenue
Leominster
Herefordshire HR6 0QF
England

Trinity Press International is a division of
the Morehouse Publishing Group.

Cover design: Brian Preuss

Library of Congress Cataloging-in-Publication Data

Kirk, J. Andrew.
    The mission of theology and theology as mission / by J. Andrew
  Kirk.
      p.   cm. – (Christian mission and modern culture series)
    Includes bibliographical references.
    ISBN 1-56338-189-3 (pbk. : alk. paper)
    1. Theology – Methodology. 2. Missions – Theory. I. Title.
  II. Series: Christian mission and modern culture.
  BR118.K618 1997
  230′.01 – dc21   96-49155
                                                                  CIP

Gracewing ISBN 0 85244 420 6

Printed in the United States of America

97   98   99   00   01   6   5   4   3   2   1

Contents

Preface to the Series

Both Christian mission and modern culture, widely regarded as antagonists, are in crisis. The emergence of the modern mission movement in the early nineteenth century cannot be understood apart from the rise of technocratic society. Now, at the end of the twentieth century, both modern culture and Christian mission face an uncertain future.

One of the developments integral to modernity was the way the role of religion in culture was redefined. Whereas religion had played an authoritative role in the culture of Christendom, modern culture was highly critical of religion and increasingly secular in its assumptions. A sustained effort was made to banish religion to the backwaters of modern culture.

The decade of the 1980s witnessed further momentous developments on the geopolitical front with the collapse of communism. In the aftermath of the breakup of the system of power blocs that dominated international relations for a generation, it is clear that religion has survived even if its institutionalization has undergone deep change and its future forms are unclear. Secularism continues to oppose religion, while technology has emerged as a major source of power and authority in modern culture. Both confront Christian faith with fundamental questions.

The purpose of this series is to probe these developments from a variety of angles with a view to helping the church understand its missional responsibility to a culture in crisis. One important resource is the church's experience of two centuries of cross-cultural mission that has reshaped the church into a global Christian *ecumene*. The focus of our inquiry will be the church in modern culture. The series (1) examines modern/postmodern culture from a missional point of view; (2) develops the theological agenda that the church in modern culture must address in order to recover its own integrity; and (3) tests fresh conceptualizations of the nature and mission of the church as it engages modern culture. In other words, these volumes are intended to be a forum where conventional assumptions can be challenged and alternative formulations explored.

This series is a project authorized by the Institute of Mennonite Studies, research agency of the Associated Mennonite Biblical Seminary, and supported by a generous grant from the Pew Charitable Trusts.

Editorial Committee

ALAN NEELY
H. WAYNE PIPKIN
WILBERT R. SHENK

1

Clearing the Ground

Introduction

The titles given to the three chapters of this volume have
been inspired by a visit some time ago to the stadium on
the top of the San Juif hill in Barcelona, before it was com-
pleted for the 1992 Olympic Games. At that time, the work
of transforming an old sports arena into one fit for a major
sporting and telecommunications event had only recently
begun. The whole interior of the old building was in the
process of being torn out, to be replaced by an entirely new
one. Only the external shell would be left of what existed
before.

The thesis of this volume is that, in a sense, the same
has to happen with the enterprise of theology and theological education, as a new millennium swiftly approaches.
On the one hand, theology in the Western world has been
constructed on intellectual assumptions that are no longer
believable; on the other hand, it is palpably inadequate to
the task that faces the Christian community worldwide at
this time. Thus, like the stadium, the old internal structures
need to be cleared away before a more serviceable model

can operate. It is even open to doubt whether the external structure itself should survive.

The set of perspectives that I want to develop in this study constitutes an ambitious and risky undertaking. I will be investigating an operation on which hangs in large part the healthy life of the whole Christian community, for if we do not get the theological task right, every other task is likely to be out of kilter. It is a topic that lies at the heart of the whole educational and training enterprise of the Christian church — one that, among other considerations, absorbs an immense amount of human and financial resources.

If we assume that the church can exist as truly itself only when dedicated to the mission of God, a burning question ensues: How should one reinvent theology and theological education so that they flow naturally from an integral perspective on God's constant will and activity in the world?[1] I do not myself stand outside this concern, having been intimately involved for the past thirty years, both in Latin America and Britain, in many different kinds of theological education. For many reasons, which I will be outlining further ahead, I believe the time has decidedly come for a sea change or, to use the current jargon, a "paradigm shift" in the way we view the whole theological enterprise.

The title of this volume points to an overwhelmingly influential heritage that has shaped theology universally — the conjunction of the Latin (*missio*) and Greek (*theos* and *logos*) languages and cultures. Now, however, the influence of the Roman and Hellenistic worlds on the subsequent development of Christian thought and practice is being challenged in many ways by Christians from the "South" who are eager to see the gospel closely related to their history and traditions.[2]

At the outset, some will probably question the association of mission with theology. They may argue that theology can be said to have various tasks, even an overall purpose, but to talk about its having a mission is dubious. Mission, it will be said, connotes undisguised commitment to a particular cause, whereas theology, traditionally understood as an academic discipline alongside its peers in other university faculties,[3] is surely a detached, careful, and tentative process of reflection.[4] I intend, in the course of this study, to show that this standard response — which understands mission as dedication to a practical calling, and theology, in the first instance, as an intellectual task — is based on inadequate assumptions. I will then show why and how theology and mission are inextricably linked, both in theory and practice.

Theology is a vast subject. In spite of the battering that it has received from secular culture, theology is still a major area of human endeavor — as evidenced, for example, by the substantial number of books published each year in this field and the immense number of theological institutions in existence across the globe. It used to be called the "Queen of Sciences," in the sense that it gave the adequate reason for the whole scientific enterprise. Though now its status in academia has been demoted, and in many institutions of higher education it has been transmuted into religious studies, it is not ignored. Over the last two hundred years its rationale and methods have changed very substantially; nevertheless, the distinct methods, motives, and content of its two-thousand-year history should be recalled at this time of reevaluation.

I do not want to limit the understanding of what constitutes theology. There are a number of different species; all, in their separate ways, have a right to be called theology. None of them can make a substantiated a priori claim to take precedence or to be wholly normative for the rest. The following headings give a rough indication of the taxonomy, or classification, of the main kinds.

Academic Study

Academic study is the model we would first naturally think of if we live in the Western world, with its strong tradition of university departments, faculties, and schools of theology. It is epitomized by the methods required to obtain a doctoral degree, by the various professional associations of scholars that determine the generally accepted conventions concerning the acceptable methods of investigation in each discipline, and by the professional theological journals that support the various disciplines. Its main symbol is probably the library.

Church-related

This type of theology might also be called "confessional theology." We have in mind the work that goes into papal encyclicals, reports of the World Council of Churches, particularly those of the Faith and Order Commission (such as *Baptism, Eucharist and Ministry* or *Confessing the Apostolic Faith Today* [Link 1987]), bilateral and multilateral statements coming from commissions set up by world communions of churches (e.g., the report that came from the Anglican Consultative Council and the World Alliance of Reformed Churches, *God's Reign and Our Unity* [1983]), and substantial affirmations of faith that emerge from world gatherings of Christians like the *Lausanne Covenant* (1974). Its symbol today is probably the conference center and the computer: the first is used to provide accommodation in the right environment for carefully selected commissions, and the second to facilitate the process of working through endless draft statements to a finally agreed-upon document.

Alternative

Alternative approaches to theology are ways of reflecting on the meaning of the Christian faith that are either outside of or critical of mainstream church theology. As examples, we might mention, among others, the oral theology of the African Independent Churches, the environmental spirituality of Matthew Fox, the ecclesiological thinking of liberation theology, the advocacy of "pluralism" as the only authentic approach to interreligious dialogue, and the promotion of the so-called prosperity gospel, which emphasizes the twin blessings of health and wealth to all who claim them in faith. Though these examples are vastly different in conception and content, they are often characterized by taking one element of the Christian tradition and pushing it to an extreme position.

Grass Roots

The best-known example of this way of doing theology would be the biblical/hermeneutical reflection going on in the base ecclesial communities (Hebblethwaite 1994:44–

76). However, it also takes place wherever and whenever ordinary Christians examine the relevance of their faith to the world around them, particularly in the exploration of ethical issues related to the various professions and to political and economic policies (Kirk 1986). Some of the most exciting theological discoveries in the world today are happening as people struggle to put the story of the gospel together with their story. For a number of years in London, I had the privilege of accompanying many people from various parts of the world in this kind of theological pilgrimage.[5]

Local

This kind of process has been mapped out most thoroughly by Robert Schreiter (1985). It is characterized particularly by prior concern with the cultural context, rather than with the received faith, as data for the theological task. Its emphasis is on the contextualization, indigenization, and enculturation of the Christian faith. There is a particularly long section in Schreiter's book on the relation of the gospel to "popular religion" in its many manifestations. The significance of this lies in the fact that religion in this form, whatever the purists might desire, is the most widely practiced variety throughout the world and has, therefore, to be taken into account in any theological reflection on the beliefs and customs of the people.

There is not always a rigorous separation between the species. We have to recognize a certain overlap in some of the cases. Nevertheless, one can detect substantially different emphases, according to the *aims* set out, the *methods* used, the *assumptions* made, the *degrees of personal commitment* expected, and the *situation* in which theology is done. These different factors have not always been given their due weight in discussions about the nature and task of theology.

Understanding the Nature and Task of Theology

There are probably almost as many definitions of the essence and intention of theology as there are people engaged in doing it.[6] Theology may be understood as scientific (*wissenschaftlich*) investigation into the texts and historical engagement of the Christian community over the centuries. The ambition of this method is to pursue detached, critical research according to the best criteria of professional scholarship (Kelsey 1993:12–27). Theology may be understood as the process whereby systematic training for church-related accredited ministries takes place and in which the traditional requirements of the different churches shape the curriculum.

Charles Wood (1985) defines theology as "critical inquiry into the validity of Christian witness." The contemporary practice of Christian communities is an essential element of the way theological reflection should happen. Orlando Costas (1986:6) believes that theology has the task of producing a faithful, obedient, missionary community, always striving to understand its vocation more adequately:

Theology [is] the reflective activity of the Christian Church that tries to understand the mystery of faith, describe its implications for life, and make visible its mission in the world.

Though I would not necessarily dissent from these explanations, my own personal understanding of theology takes a different focus and can be outlined as follows:

> It is a reflective, intellectual process carried out by a community of faith whose concern is with God and his relationship to the entire universe. This process gives a privileged place to certain sources of knowledge, namely, the Bible, the ecumenical creeds, and other historical confessions of faith. It has two fundamental tasks: to make sense of the whole of life by reference to God, and to be an agent of the transformation of the whole of life so that it may reflect God's intentions.[7]

Later in this study I will elaborate on these two main tasks — or overall mission — of theology, as I see them. However, for reasons that have to do with its potential for standing in the way of a fresh calling for theology, there is a need to look critically at the academic model of theology. This model has had a dominating, almost exclusive, influence for a period of about two hundred years, during which time it has assumed the right to be the arbiter of good and bad theology, valuing more highly its own methods of rigorous criticism over all other types of theological work. Moreover, academic theology per se might well reject both tasks, outlined above, as necessary definitions of theology's aims and objectives.

Theology done within the confines of the academy has appeared to operate according to criteria different from those presupposed in the definition I have suggested above. It has tended to concentrate on an analytical, interpretative, and reconstructive process concerned mainly with the linguistic forms of original texts, their genre, their original historical context, and the mode of their transmission through various stages of mutation till they came to rest in their final historical setting. Basic to this mode of investigation are these questions: What did the text mean? In what context was it written? What parallels with other texts can be suggested? What effect did it have? All of these questions have to do with the past.

By scrutinizing the fruit of academic study, one would adduce that the scholarly ideal has been to leave the present behind and, through imagination and the creative use of data, immerse oneself in past realities. It is not surprising, then, that theology has relied so heavily on the renowned historical-critical method. Even where new approaches have arisen that concentrate on the finished text or on transpositional, hermeneutical considerations, the method remains pervasive.

I believe that much, though by no means all, of this work is a basic resource for theology, *but it is not theology itself.* Nor is what often happens as a next stage — namely, the comparative process of bringing the ideas and beliefs of others (i.e., secondary sources) into parallel lines, as it were, in order to discuss different interpretative theories.[8]

Theology, to be theology, must have a personal dimension oriented to the present: that is, to personal, openly declared preferences involving engagement and commitment, including a solid identification with the Christian community. One overriding reason for this, often spelled out, but not yet sufficiently heeded, is that the major *object* of the reflective task — God, or the Word of God, in relation to the universe — is also the *subject* who calls, makes demands, and sets tasks. In other words, in the course of study it is impossible to remain detached from the evident fact that the text presents us with a living God who calls us to be part of his righteous rule *on God's terms.*

The interpreter cannot remain detached from the message of the text, in a kind of cocoon of suspended judgment. For the attempt to remain free from any interaction with the text as communication is already a judgment about one's method and one's relation to the particular configuration of words. As a consequence, I have never understood how it is possible to study the text of the Bible as if it were just another piece of literature from the Ancient Near East, for it manifestly is not — both on the grounds of its content (the prophetic demand for repentance, conversion, and change) and the impact of its message (turning around the lives of individuals, communities, and whole cultures).[9]

Perhaps the fundamentally assumed object-subject distinction is what distinguishes religious studies as a phenomenological pursuit from theology proper. The study of religion as a discipline has its own rationale and method. However, even here both the nature of religious communities in the modern world and what they claim about their religious beliefs make this far from being a purely dispassionate study undertaken by an isolated thinking subject. There is also the relevant question of the motivation that leads the individual to choose to undertake study in this particular field. To pretend that rigorous research can take place in any subject (even the exact sciences) independently of assumed human preferences and ideals is now an old-fashioned and quite illusory myth (Barbour 1990:chap. 2).

Only an ingenuous dreamer could imagine that the pursuit of intellectual knowledge as a disinterested operation, having purely theoretical goals, is possible.

For a number of reasons, however, it seems to be hard for the academic community to recognize the dimension of "subject" in its work of investigation — that is, that the text confronts us, not so much that we confront the text. First, the methods of study used have traditionally been aligned with the natural sciences, reflecting a desire to be counted a legitimate part of the universal rational program of the academy, whose characteristic method has been that of observation by the seeing eye from outside, through the microscope or the telescope. (In the case of theology, the eye looks not at cells and galaxies but at texts from the past.) Second, the assumption that research can be done by unconditioned individuals from an unbiased basis has been widely accepted. In this sense, theological knowledge is believed to be

> publicly accessible to any interested person who has the necessary competencies. Indeed, as the result of disciplined and orderly critical inquiry, it is supposed to be accessible independent of any prejudices or special interests of either the researcher or competent observer (Kelsey 1993:25).

Third, though perhaps unconsciously, the Cartesian dualism, which postulates an imagined isolated thinking subject able to explore the world, as if emerging from a cave for the first time, has been treated as a true account of all rational endeavor.

In contrast to these presuppositions, I believe that theology has to begin from a fundamentally different location. Although the following claims may seem somewhat scandalous in the context of the pursuit of academic excellence, I am convinced they are more easily defensible, partly because of their theological integrity and partly because they are truer to what happens in practice, than those that underlie the hitherto generally accepted academic model.

In the first place, *belief is prior to understanding* (*credo et intelligo*). The first act of theology is to believe and trust that the core of what the Christian community has always held to be the case is valid. In a sense, theology is a sacramental act in which one's own baptismal vows are being constantly reaffirmed. Or, to argue from a secular perspective, our very experience of being human obliges us to acknowledge that a faith stance prior to and pervading all intellectual work (e.g., in deducing criteria to test truth claims) is inevitable.

In the second place, *grace is prior to works*. Understanding, distinct from both information and knowledge, is, first and foremost, a gift from above; it is not primarily the result of heroic human exertion (Matt. 11:25–27).[10] Hence, the oft-repeated phrase "the pursuit of truth" as a human task or achievement is unreal and illogical. Unless truth is already given, or assumed, there is no means of knowing when it has been discovered! Truth is received, not hunted in order to be preserved as if it were an endangered species!

In the third place, and this will be even more controversial, *submission to God's word is prior to intellectual freedom*. Whatever might be argued theoretically, in practice the choice is stark, though real: either one submits to the ex-

ternal authority of God's word written or one submits to
another authority. This latter may be to one's own or someone else's reason, as in the whole project of modernity, or to
the authority of feelings and experience, as in postmodern
belief. In the last two cases there can be no doubt that the
same processes are at work as in the first — the selection by
faith of an external authority and an implicit submission to
its criteria.

The idea of freedom as a state or stance without bound-
aries and wholly impervious to the (often hidden) coercion
of cultural expectations, which confine choice, is another
modern illusion. It is fascinating to note how the word of
Jesus Christ has been totally reversed by the expectations of
modern epistemology. He claimed that "if you continue in
my teaching . . . you will know the truth, and the truth will
make you free" (John 8:32). Modern human reason says,
"if you reject all authoritative assertions, you will indeed be
free, and the freedom will lead you to truth."

The Illusory Claims
of Traditional Academic Theology

In the light of these general, introductory remarks, I would
like to survey a number of inherent, methodological defi-
ciencies in the academic model of theology. This will be
prior to setting theology in a much wider context and coming to ways of working that do justice to the integrity of
theology, when allowed to be true to its own rationale,
rather than being confined within a logic that alienates it
from its proper foundation.

The academic model is based on the unreal claim to be a scientific method. It is hard to know what is the status of this oft-repeated claim, but as an analogy to the disciplines of the natural sciences, the academic model does not fit. However, it does not, as a result, have any less intellectual honor than subjects that are studied according to other criteria. It is simply the case that different methods are appropriate to different subjects.

The scientific method begins with a universally accepted assumption (or, in current terminology, faith commitment) that the processes of the natural world function in a regular or uniform way (e.g., that our blood will be pumped round our body in the same direction tomorrow as it is today). It proceeds then by imagination, by which the scientist proposes certain hypotheses ("what if . . . "). The central work, following from this, is that of testing the *hypotheses* by carefully *regulated experiments,* according to universally accepted *criteria.* The final phase is that of the *verification* of hypotheses (e.g., that smoking leads to a deterioration of health, that obesity is caused by eating fatty foods, or that increased emissions of carbon dioxide in the atmosphere produce the phenomenon called "global warming") to establish whether they should be accepted, modified, or abandoned.[11]

Science deals with the kind of data that is, in principle, susceptible to being directly investigated. Theology cannot apply the same methodology because the nature of the data is fundamentally different and because there are no universally accepted criteria for testing. In one sense, the only thing theology has in common with science is hypotheses. The ascription of "scientific" to the methods that theology uses ought to be dropped because they receive thereby, within a particular cultural framework, an undeserved aura and sense of invincibility.

In practice, in much theological scholarship, particularly in the field of biblical studies, the necessary relationship between theory, substantive evidence, rigorous testing, and conclusion is tenuous. Much too much is built on unproven (and probably unprovable) conjecture. Perhaps this is one reason why fashions in scholarship can appear and disappear on a seasonal basis. Like trends in clothes, they originate in the creative imagination of the fashion designer, only to be replaced the following year by something even more wondrous than the style that had gone before.

Academic theology's pretensions to being a genuinely critical method are suspect. In traditional academic theology, the historical-critical method has been the bedrock of any work able to claim intellectual rigor and credibility. In accordance with certain Enlightenment emphases, out of which it grew, the method begins with a first principle of doubt (or suspicion). Thus the historical accounts of the biblical narrative are assumed to be guilty of exaggeration or of reconstructing stories to fit a predetermined theological stance, until proved innocent. The principle of "Occam's razor" is also used against the prima facie account of the text.

In my estimation, in this whole procedure skepticism has been disastrously confused with criticism. For two hundred years or so theological faculties and departments have gone about their work under the illusion that the critical method is an impregnable fortress from which we may sally forth to do battle with all kinds of theological naïveté, fundamentalism, and other forms of strong Christian belief in the accessibility of final truth. The assumption is made that there is a clear divide between a critical and a confessional approach to theology:

> Only after critical testing do we have true "knowledge." "Intellectual intuition" and "reason" are strictly separated, and only human capacities for critical, disciplined, orderly problem-solving in the framework of research agendas, or other situations approximating such research agendas, count as "rationality" (Kelsey 1993:27).

It is this confusion, perhaps more than anything else, that has led to a certain schizophrenia between academic pursuits, on the one hand, and spirituality, mission, and pastoral concerns, on the other. In many cases the divide is imagined, for the critical method has to presuppose a particular vantage point that is itself not exempt from criticism from other vantage points; and none of them can claim a priori a superior rational standing. It is for this reason, also, that convinced belief cannot necessarily be equated with naïveté.

One of the aims of the critical method has been the partly justifiable goal of wanting to distinguish between unassailable historical fact and ideologically convenient interpretations of history.[12] It has sought to fulfill this objective by the onion-skin process of stripping away alleged layers of biased material in the belief that it must be possible to lay bare a core of unprejudiced facts. That is why so much theological investigation proceeds by conjecture and reconstruction.

In more skeptical hands, however, doubt is erected into an article of faith (beyond mere method) — a negative belief, starting from a series of propositions that, as is often popularly stated, "cannot any longer be believed by modern, rational people." What specifically cannot be believed are miracles, because presumably the absolute uniformity of nature is more believable than God's special action to achieve specific ends.[13]

The method, therefore, often assumes the doctrine (or dogma) of naturalism[14] as a necessary starting point for a truly critical process. The problem, however, is obvious to all who have not succumbed to the theory: the assumption on which it is built has to be accepted as incontrovertibly self-evident and, therefore, made immune from doubt and criticism.

Of course, there is a proper historical approach (often more clearly spelled out by professional historians than by theologians) whose proper task is to illuminate the meaning of texts by reference to historical location. As Eric Ives says, "The analogy closest to the activity of the historian is the detection and trial of a crime. What matters is what the evidence is worth. The historical goal is probability. . . . The role of the historian is to achieve the highest level of probability congruent with the state of the evidence" (1992:19–20). Another way of putting the matter would be in terms of the instruction given to juries that they can bring in a verdict only when the evidence convinces them of the guilt or innocence of the defendant "beyond all reasonable doubt." According to the widely accepted principle of fairness, in the absence of such evidence the accused remains innocent and the prosecution's case is declared unproven.

There is a growing tendency to use theology as a transmitter of symbolic significancies. Inevitably, the doubt-inspired method of historical criticism has led to a culture of skepticism. But, as it is impossible to doubt all propositions simultaneously, a new search for meaning through the use of texts is going on. No longer are some theologians concerned with the original significance, which is generally considered to be archaic and anachronistic, but with the "significance-for-me" or "significance-for-us." The two levels of meaning — the original and the contemporary — do not need to have any continuity at all.

This process adopts, consciously or unconsciously, the "deconstructionist" dogma that texts have to be read in the understanding that there is no meta-narrative (either the historical-Christian or the universal-rational) that has any basis for indicating, or even illuminating, what it means to be human. The poet Michael O'Siadhail uses the phrase "never again one voice" to capture the mood of revolt against the kind of all-embracing theories that have led in the twentieth century to the "utopias" of communism, national socialism, and autonomous-market capitalism or to the comprehensive certainties of religious fundamentalisms.[15] Not only the Christian, but the liberal-humanist worldview, is deemed irrecoverable. We, as autonomous subjects, now have to give ourselves the freedom to decide which meaning from the text we will accept, or to create our own individual meaning.[16]

The method fits the mood of the times almost perfectly.

It is a "consumer-approach" to theology:[17] I construct out
of my experience whatever I choose. The text becomes a
tool for shaping the history of the individual, the group, or
the whole species in ways that seem personally liberating,
contextually significant, and culturally self-evident. The assumption is made clear that one can live with integrity in
the modern world only by accepting the equal validity of
a multiplicity of different religious views. The "one voice"
is identified negatively with the struggle of certain communities to secure for themselves a dominating or controlling
place within society:

> It is very difficult to give material content to the
> idea of an "essence" that unifies schooling without its
> becoming dangerously open to ideological distortion.
> The danger of proceeding in this way is that one may
> unify theological schooling but in doing so may hide
> larger inequities in the arrangement of social power
> and may validate particular oppressive arrangements
> of power (Kelsey 1993:224–5).

Of course, the method reverses the age-long tradition
that human beings found perfect meaning and freedom in
listening obediently to God's word written (*the* "one voice").
Now the text is to be conquered and shaped so that it pro-
vides "mythological" support for beliefs and actions deemed
right on quite other grounds. Life is to be a celebration
of the many voices that contribute to the universal store-
house of meaning and value. Sundermeier, in his response
to the missiological thinking of David Bosch, illustrates this
process very well:

> Texts are "open" in the sense that they constantly invite renewed and deepened interpretation. They are like works of art in that they only acquire meaning in the process of reception. In passing through the understanding recipient they are changed.... In this process of understanding the message changes (Kritzinger and Saayman 1990:263).

Because of the strong drift of contemporary Western culture toward anarchy of belief systems, it may yet take a long time before the manifold problems of this method are recognized. Though the consequence, as is already evident, will be a steady slide into irrationality, isolation, and meaninglessness, what fits comfortably into a cultural consensus among certain groups in society is not easily dislodged by argument. Orlando Costas (1986:15) argues that a pluralist approach to theology undermines its missiological possibilities, because it sanctions theological provincialism. If situation is the supreme criterion for the utmost integrity in theological construction, there are no grounds for distinguishing between opinions that emerge out of particular, isolated, individual, and subjective judgments about the rightness of beliefs and actions:

> Academia needs to take seriously the problem of how to relinquish a claim on a set body of knowledge as somehow containing the "truth," without succumbing in the process to every current and tide of new expression (Smith 1993:96).

One is inclined to say: Exactly so! The pluralist thesis about diversity and the contingency of all beliefs, on the ground that they are historically conditioned, makes an interesting theory, but it cannot work in practice. Action springs from commitment to particular beliefs and objectives. If people held, at all moments, that these were entirely provisional, their decisions would become totally paralyzed by an all-encompassing uncertainty and apprehension. Moreover, and perhaps more seriously, consistent pluralism renders all resistance to manifest evil innocuous.[18] Therefore, neither textual interpretation nor the general task of theological reflection can possibly sidestep the always prior question of truth.

There is a general confusion about aims and objectives. Academic theology has thrived on the false distinction between "doing theology," with its implied perspective and committed interaction with living reality, and teaching and studying theology, with its implied disinterested, impartial presentation of a variety of viewpoints.

The dichotomy can best be summed up, perhaps, by the nature of what is required to achieve the higher, academic degree: the test of excellence and competence lies in what is known, who is quoted, and how one argues, not in what one believes (this may be highly suspect and therefore should be bracketed out) or what kind of action is required. An illustration of this would be the experience of a friend in defending his doctoral thesis on the phenomenon of the "Messianic Jews:" neither the pattern of his research nor the conclusions he drew from the data assembled were particularly put in question; only his own conviction, which informed his work throughout, that the existence of "Messianic Jews" was a legitimate result of a justifiable evangelistic approach to Jewish people.[19] The expectation of the examiners was that a critical approach to the study should end in a noncommitted stance. Only a little reflection, however, shows that in a case like this, belief of one kind or another cannot be suspended, for one has to accept that, according to prior convictions, evangelism and conversion are either legitimate or not. Even a person who might maintain a stance of indifference to the question does so on the basis of other beliefs.

Of course, those who are engaged in serious theological reflection must proceed by acknowledging, analyzing, and facing objections to their own views and, if persuaded by the weight of evidence or the arguments put forward, must change or modify them. Such a procedure, however, is a long way from admitting that there is any difference in kind between theological work done in a strictly "nonconfessional" academic environment and in the confessionally committed locale of a seminary or college whose purpose is to train leaders for Christian communities.

In terms of Kelsey's disjunction between "Athens" and "Berlin," the distinction between a method that strives to inculcate the tools necessary to pursue theological inquiry as a disinterested intellectual exercise and that which seeks to form people theologically, pastorally, ethically, and spiritually within a particular tradition cannot be sustained. The simple and obvious reality is that the mind cannot be separated from the person and his or her history and context. It is much better, therefore, for all approaches to theology to admit the particular commitment from which they begin.

2

Building the Stadium

Factors Pushing the Enterprise in New Directions

Starting with a brief summary of the discussion so far, I will list some of the main factors that are pushing the whole enterprise of theology into new directions.

The Inadequacy of the Existing Paradigm

The combined weight of Michael Polanyi's thesis of "tacit knowing," in his work on the methodology of science (1958), and the insights coming from the sociology of knowledge that knowing is socially constructed have led to the recognition that those who are engaged in a discipline like theology cannot stand outside in a zone protected from the subtle influence of personal beliefs and interests. They cannot act as if they were umpires arbitrating in a tennis match, elevated above the arena of play — final judges of the way the rules of the game are to be interpreted. It is impossible, therefore, to move from some kind of sanitized, unideological, "pure thought" to its application to events in the everyday world.

The theologian is already committed in all sorts of ways both before and during the pursuit of his or her craft. It is liberating to recognize this, for everyone is in the same situation. No one is more or less biased than anyone else. Each has particular preferences that show in different ways. One cannot, for example, rule out the way that the benefits to be gained from the academic teaching of theology influence the results of one's study. There is great pressure on those whose livelihood is bound up with their tenure in a university teaching post to conform to particular intellectual conventions. The maverick who consistently steps out of line with the established norms of academically approved performance is unlikely to go far. However, only those with a simple and naïve faith in academic neutrality could imagine that such norms are unquestionably valid or that it is possible to suspend belief (and what they have in mind is usually someone else's belief, rarely their own) while engaged in the pursuit of knowledge and understanding.

It follows from this, I believe, that all theology should begin with a "proto-theological" phase in which the theologian is prepared to reveal and discuss all hidden assumptions, and a general kind of health warning is given against all pretensions of the academy to a universally valid vantage point. One example of the way in which unexamined assumptions come to supplant open processes of reasoning is the dispute about the plenary inspiration of Scripture. There are, in the nature of the case, no facts, historical or otherwise, nor any universally accepted, rational norm that obliges all intelligent beings to accept, in this case, one position rather than another. We may weigh the evidence and accept for ourselves the probability of one position, but the factors that influence us are often cultural in the wide sense and may be unconscious. Indeed, the less we are aware of the conditioning force of extraneous factors, the more likely we are to be influenced by them.

Thus, not to believe in the plenary inspiration of Scripture is just as much a matter of disposition or inclination as to believe in it. Each carries all the weight of an a priori faith commitment. Ridiculing another's belief is no substitute for substantive argument. And yet, what chance would an otherwise highly qualified person, who admitted to believing in the full inspiration of the text of Scripture, have to secure an academic post in a university? Why should only certain kinds of belief be deemed acceptable or unacceptable? Would there not be a terrible outcry among "advanced" thinkers if a person who denied the plenary inspiration of Scripture was rejected, on this ground alone, from being a candidate for a teaching post in a "conservative" college? Would this not be condemned by more "enlightened" people as unacceptable discrimination, even as having contravened "equal opportunity" principles? To take seriously and to be rigorously honest about every kind of bias is the first step toward helping theology in general to be more widely self-critical than it is at present.

A Recognition of the Necessity to Rethink Educational Practices

Possibly, because there has been a tendency in recent years for more mature students to study theology, there is gradually emerging a greater willingness to involve them in the whole process of their own education than has been the case formerly. It is now more widely recognized that programs that serve first the needs of the educator, and into which the learners must fit, are pedagogically and ethically inadmissible. In the institution where I am involved in mission education, we try not to use the term student for those coming to learn, but rather, participant. The idea is to use language to signify the educational ideal — that education is about processes of learning in which all, the tutor and the tutee, participate.

At the same time, the educational method highlighted by liberation theology of "see, judge, act" is also gaining currency. In engaging the participant much more in a whole process of observation, discernment, decision making, and action, the balance between the input of the expert and of previous experience and practice will be changed, lessening the control of the first. In this way we move from a teacher-centered model to a learner-centered model. The teacher's task is to be a facilitator, a resource, and a stimulus, helping participants to relate gospel, church, and world in critical and creative ways.[20]

The advent of the "information highway" has given rise to new concepts of the resources that educational establishments need in order to maximize the potential of participants to be involved as subjects of their own learning processes. Access to the varied forms of computer technology now becoming available should mean that much less attention is given to the classical lecture, even perhaps to classroom activity that involves the use of multimedia presentations and discussion. The future of adult education is likely to be conducted among the three points: the learning resource center, exposure/placements, and the tutorial group.

The Incursion of Theological Thought from the South

Whatever we may think of liberation theology, there is a sense in which we now live in a post-liberation theology age.[21] I will consider some of the major concerns that have begun to transform the whole enterprise of theology from the perspective of the "South."

Owing to a growing awareness in the postcolonial era of the perennial identification of the church and its theological underpinning with politically conservative and oppressive regimes, theologians have applied Marx's famous dictum about the practice of philosophy to theology. Thus:

> The [theologians] have only *interpreted* the world, in various ways; the point, however, is to *change* it (*Theses on Feuerbach*, No. XI).

The impossibility of separating intellectual work from life commitments, either by commission or omission, leads inevitably to a critique of Western intellectual assumptions. Western theology is interpreted as one part, even though this has been obscured by its claims to universality, of Western colonial expansion. The present world order, characterized by the North-South divide and the fragmentation of peoples in many parts of Africa, Asia, and Latin America — and not forgetting postcold war Europe — into artificially constructed nation states, belongs to a history imposed from outside. This is why people from the South speak of living on the "underside" (in Spanish the word means literally "the reverse" side) of history.

Dominant industrialized societies are almost incapable of forgoing a certain "messianic" pretentiousness about being able to solve all problems everywhere. Peoples of the

South, quite rightly, are mightily unimpressed by the state of Western societies and say, "Physician, heal yourself!" Yet the deeply felt superiority of Western culture and civilization (the norm of being a "civilized" society) dies hard. One can see in this an absurd, even manic, obsession with the benefits of one particular economic system and how consumer choice has become the chief criterion for defining human identity.[22]

Theology, unfortunately, has participated in this sense of superiority in spite of the fact, seen clearly from the South, that Western theology has hardly begun seriously to challenge Western culture. One of the interesting results of the proposals put forward by Lesslie Newbigin (1990; 1991) — in his desire to test the thesis that, because "the Gospel is public truth," one of the major missionary tasks of the church in the West is to call the culture to conversion to the gospel — is the sharp and even angry reactions that his writings quite often receive. It is as if some Christians, by showing themselves to be overly defensive, hold that modern Western culture, as the result of a certain, unquestioned way of thinking and being, is sacrosanct. It may be questioned at the margins, but not at the center of its core assumptions, for then the "emperor," that is, the new imperium, would lose his clothes and his ugly nakedness would be exposed. Newbigin, quite unjustifiably in my opinion, is then accused of wanting to turn the culture-clock back to an imagined era when culture was friendly toward and supportive of Christian beliefs and values,[23] by trying to reclaim the public square in the name of the gospel.

The doyens of the interreligious theological scene, such

as John Hick and Wilfred Cantwell Smith, openly acknowledge their indebtedness to the dualism of Greek thought and the rational dichotomy of Kant's philosophical scheme — in other words, to powerful strands of Western cultural history. Challenge this influence in the name of an alternative intellectual heritage and their particular rational structure collapses. Surely, at the heart of its view of the world, Christian faith challenges two cardinal assumptions of Greek philosophy and its subsequent intellectual tradition: the distinction between sacred and profane realms of reality and the separation of reality into the phenomenologically contingent and the noumenally absolute worlds. In other words, Christianity can be true to itself only when it is prepared to disengage itself from some of the central thought forms of the Hellenistic culture.

To the question, Wherein lies the validation of the plausibility of the gospel message? Western theology is likely to say with the criteria of the modern (or now for some the postmodern) mind: Does it conform to accepted standard norms? Theological thinkers from the South will answer quite differently, putting the emphasis on its missionary effectiveness; that is, its ability to inspire people to be agents and embodiments of the life of God's new creation in Jesus Christ. If the latter are correct, then theology's main purpose is to elucidate in different situations the imperatives of the *missio Dei* and the *missio ecclesiae.*

The Recognition That the Western World Poses the Greatest Contemporary Missionary Challenge to the Church

This dawning of consciousness has been immensely slow in coming because of countervailing tendencies like the sheer inertia of ecclesiastical structures (which, like the great oil tankers, need much time and space to turn around) and the deeply powerful pastoral model of ministry, inherited from the past. The Church of England, for example, with which I am particularly familiar, behaves like an institution dominated by a rural mentality, though ostensibly engaged in urban ministry.

Mission historian Andrew Walls says that up to the present "the missionary movement has always been considered as an extension of the church at the margins."[24] In other words, mission always takes place somewhere where the church is not already established. This view has been in part the long and deep legacy of the 1910 Edinburgh World Missionary Conference, with its strong distinction between the Christian and the non-Christian worlds. At the same time, in the West the more vigorous evangelistic work of the church in the United States of America, compared to that going on in Europe, may be because of the tenacity with which European Christians have bought into, and still in many instances continue to defend, the "territorial principle" of established churches, whose mission work is still based on the assumption that the European peoples are implicitly Christian, rather than being overtly pagan.[25]

The response to the "Decade of Evangelism" shows that there is a great confusion in Europe about the missionary task and how to implement it. Ordinary Christian people point to a need to regain confidence in the truth and power of the Christian message, whereas many of their leaders confess to knowing more about what the gospel is not than what it is. Andrew Walls has also put forward a theory of church history as consisting of great missionary ebbs and flows. The ebb in Europe is patently obvious, particularly among the young, a fact constantly remarked on by Christians visiting from Africa, Asia, and Latin America. Perhaps there has to be yet further decline before the church will be prepared to countenance any radically new responses, not least in the area of theological education. For example, as well as among the young, the challenge to communicate the gospel to a "nonliterate" or "semiliterate" culture is a matter that requires deeply serious theological exploration.

The Two Tasks of Theology

I will now elaborate further the two major tasks, or mission, of theology that I stated programmatically in Chapter 1 and will test their validity.

To Make Sense of the Whole of Life by Reference to God

I agree with the central emphasis of liberation theology that concepts of God are absolutely central to all theological work (Munoz 1991:3–14). At its heart the faith of the Bible is prophetic: of the three mediators of God's word highlighted in the Old Testament — priest, prophet, and wise person — the prophet speaks with the greatest clarity and forcefulness about the nature and intentions of God. Moreover, the word of the true prophet is least able to be manipulated by religious or political elites in the interests of maintaining intact their privileges over against the clamor of the disinherited.

Theology, if it is going to be anything other than the esoteric pastime of a small professional coterie, must recapture the centrality of the prophetic word for its task. Here, however, it may find itself in somewhat of a dilemma on two scores. On the one hand, emphasis on the Word has been associated for most of this century with the "dialectical" theology of Karl Barth; and though he was a master theological craftsman, no contemporary reconstruction of theology should, by an association of language, be aligned immediately with that of someone else, however brilliant.

Barth has a reputation for having developed a theology in which the transcendent communication of God is in sharp discontinuity with human-constructed cultural effects. This emphasis tends to negate the impact of the prophetic message, because its forcefulness is in direct relation to its ability to penetrate to the heart of a culture, deliver its message there, and be heard as judgment, warning, and promise. Too sharp a separation of the word from the world may imply that the former becomes incomprehensible to the latter. The prophet, then, would not be so much "crying in the wilderness" as "proclaiming into a void." The message of Jeremiah, Jonah, and Jesus was clearly understood, even when it was morally unacceptable to some of those who heard. Barth's dialectical theology is less than helpful when reflecting on the pressing necessity to communicate the meaning of God to a generation that has lost touch.

A theology of the word has also been part of the evangelical tradition of the church. Unlike Barth, many evangelicals have deeply imbibed the Reformation belief that God's special revelation is transparent to those who are open to hear its message. The gap between the mind of God and the minds of men and women is not as great as Barth gives the impression of believing. Nevertheless, modern culture finds it difficult to take the evangelical witness seriously. Many commentators pick on certain characteristics — like the supposed need to possess spiritual certainty, the appeal to moral absolutes, the rejection of certain scientific theories such as evolution, and the bizarre, literalistic interpretations of the Bible made by some — as evidence of a precritical, premodern mentality.

A rediscovery of the centrality of the word of God in its faithful communication through prophet and apostle has to be freed from association either with dialectical theology or with the triumphalistic gospel, and the simplistic exegetical methods adopted by some conservative groups of Christians. Liberation theology may provide another perspective. It is not tainted by the kind of negative views of theologies of the word noted above, and yet, because it also insists that God is knowable through his word, it too is decidedly a theology of the word (Shaull 1991).

On the other hand, certain strands of modern thinking are deeply suspicious of the "Word" and words. It is assumed in postmodern literary theory that words, particularly when allied to truth claims, have the totalizing effect of imposing an absolute prohibition on all forms of difference. Thus theology, which insists on the givenness of the word of God and the non-negotiability of the narrative of the Word, is dismissed as a dissimulated will-to-power: "never again one voice!"

"A Theology of the Word" thus has a difficult task, both in relation to the past dialectical emphasis on the profound break between the Word and culture and to the present deconstructionist insistence on the break between culture and all universal words.

Nevertheless, it is urgent that theology recover a self-conscious mission to contemporary culture to help arrest its further slide into the abyss of nihilism. As John Milbank (1990:261–62) says: "All modern, critical thought is itself under suspicion of being a will-to-power.... Post-modern suspicion leaves no residue of secure, humanist meaning."

It is not surprising that this generation has seen a resurgence of interest in Nietzsche. As Allan Bloom (1987:143) says, in his trenchant critique of the mindless contemporary cult of open-mindedness and tolerance above all things:

Nietzsche with the utmost gravity told modern man that he was free-falling in the abyss of nihilism.... Nobody really believes in anything any more, and everyone spends his life in frenzied work and frenzied play so as not to face the fact, not to look into the abyss.

Anyone aware of the gravity of the present crisis of culture, and concerned about its destructive human consequences, should welcome the call of Newbigin and others to a missionary encounter with contemporary culture.[26] There are two major areas that have to be tackled, both of which profoundly affect the sense of meaninglessness that characterizes this generation and the possibility of recovering again an adequate basis for meaning. First, there is the inability of a world, dominated by scientific culture, to comprehend human life in any way other than by reference to biological origins and the final physiological destiny of deterioration, death, and disintegration. The insistence of referring everything to nature (quite deliberately chosen as a word in contrast to "creation") has led to the deep oppression of life experienced as imprisonment in a mechanistic universe (Yu 1987:115–43). The loss of an overarching teleology, which would restore purpose to human existence, is an exorbitant price to pay for banishing God to the realm of personal and private opinion and experience.

Second, there is the present intoxication with pluralism. The hermeneutic of suspicion finds an ontological imperialism in every claim to universal validity. This finds expression in the apparently self-evident, cultural relativity of all our views. This leads further to a kind of cultural positivism, which affirms that every culture is right, because it is. Such a view is held to be particularly true in respect of minority cultures, because, without doubt, they have often been brutally suppressed by other conquering cultures.[27]

Our age wants to celebrate the relativism of all perspectives. We live now "beyond good and evil," even though, as Bloom points out, that gives us severe difficulties with making sense of human rights. The current emphasis on cultural diversity, as an end in itself, may be one way of trying to escape from the impasse of scientism and get a toe back into teleology, on the basis that cultures, by their very nature, cohere through commonly shared ends.

The globalization of theological education, which has become something of a fashion within progressive theological circles, seems to draw a lot of its inspiration from the imperative to recognize the benefits that accrue from celebrating a pluralism of cultures.[28] What appears to be self-evidently true, namely, that Western cultural/theological hegemony must be destroyed, by demonstrating its imperialistic and humiliating effects, in the hands of some theologians actually becomes a reinforcement of the status quo.

The convictions and commitments of Christians living in other parts of the world can be accepted as a witness to the truth of the gospel, whose implication is that we in the West should repent of our blindness, hypocrisy, and unfaithfulness, and change our views and our missionary and pastoral practice. It is certainly the intent of some who have embarked on a process of globalization that the possibility of such an outcome be squarely faced. On the other hand, globalization can be construed as the celebration of an incommensurable variety of different stances, which forces Western theology to recognize its cultural limitations and parochialism, obliges it to desist from criticizing other theological positions, but otherwise leaves it basically unchallenged, secure in its culturally relative cocoon. Schreiter (1993:127) delineates the problem that multiplicity continually poses:

> One way of answering the multiplicity question owes a great deal to the dominant culture in North America where an ideology of plurality (as opposed to pluralism) is cultivated. In this ideology, no unity or universality is sought, since that might be construed as the triumph of one view over the others. Rather, a plurality is maintained, wherein all are allowed to coexist, *provided that none threatens the existence or well-being of the other* [my emphasis].... In theological education, in an interest to help students and faculty see the diversity of culture and of God's world, we can sometimes fudge a bit the questions

of universality, dismissing them as signs of anxiety or intransigence.

Thus the acknowledgment of a polycentric world can either enable the prophetic word of the gospel to penetrate more deeply through the shell of resistance to its life-changing message, or it can hold it off at a safe distance, out of range of our secure, culturally autonomous bunker.

I believe that, like the way some handle the question of cultural multiplicity, the present fascination with the pluriformity of religious convictions and practices among some theologians and the attempt to construct a viable theology of pluralism are also related to the refusal to countenance one, universally valid, prophetic word that comprehensively tells us who we are and what we are to become. Robert Charles Zaehner, former professor of Eastern Religions and Ethics at the University of Oxford, began his tenure in the chair as a convinced believer in the uniqueness and finality of Christ among the religions, but finished by laying the blame for the ills of Western society (and the rest) at the feet of the prophetic faith of the Judeo-Christian tradition and advocating in its place the stance of Zen Buddhism and other examples of philosophical mysticism, beyond reason, revelation, and ethical norms (*The Listener* 1970). His own intellectual trajectory mirrors that of the society to which he belonged. Like so many others, he was, apparently, unable to withstand the relentless Zeitgeist of his day.

The mission of both Old Testament prophet and New Testament apostle was carried on in a social milieu not dissimilar to our own: there was a substantial period of political stability in the eighth-century kingdoms of Israel and Judah and in the first-century Roman Empire, leading to economic prosperity and, in turn, to religious pluralism. Idolatry, to use the prophets' characterization of the religion of their time, was both commercially profitable and religiously necessary. The false prophets and soothsayers were paid handsomely for their encouragement to neglect the terms of the covenant and despise the warnings of impending doom. In the New Testament we have the example of the silversmiths of Ephesus.

> Demetrius saw clearly, as did the practitioners of magic, that a choice had to be made between Jesus and the new order of things which he represented and the common religious beliefs that the ordinary people had hitherto practised. Unlike some modern global religious ecumenists, they did not envisage any way of bringing the faith of Jesus and the faith of Artemis into some kind of creative harmony (Kirk 1992:156).

In both cases religion is the occasion for and the legitimating power of corrupt business practices. On a pluralist view, however, the religions should not be questioned at their very core.

Our pluralist world, then, is oscillating dangerously between what would be, if believed and acted on, the prophetic word that destroys idols and brings life from the dead — and the immensely confusing babble of words. Because there is no basis for discernment, an insidious creeping mood of cultural doubt and paralysis is gripping all Western societies. I maintain it is a significant task of theology to persuade — not to coerce — our generation to listen again to the Word in order to be able to make sense of the contemporary confusion of words.

To Be an Agent of Transformation, So That the Whole of Life May Reflect God's Intentions

Solid, disciplined, and prolonged intellectual work in the context of a missionary encounter between the gospel and contemporary cultures is an essential part of the mission of theology. To fulfill such a task, it has to be much more self-critical of its tendency to acquiesce in whatever happens to be the currently ascendant worldview. It has, from its own "autonomous" roots, in the sense of being independent of the traditional Western metaphysical dichotomy between reason and revelation, to develop its own integral hermeneutic of suspicion.

Though admittedly not a straightforward assignment, the apostolic message of Jesus has within itself the implements necessary for distinguishing between corrupt and corrupting ideologies and beliefs and actions that genuinely free people to be and do as God intended. It is able to act in this way because it challenges both the assumption that listening to the cacophony of many voices is the most certain way to discover truth and goodness, and that the single, direct voice is automatically imperialist and oppressive. Within the word of Jesus there is a perfect combination of truth and freedom (Kirk forthcoming: chap. 9).

However, it is crucial to the integrity of theology never to isolate its intellectual work from the call to be a force for the transformation of human life, so that it might be remade in the image of Christ, who is "the (visible) image of the invisible God" (Col. 1:15). This is the message of theology from the South, from the "margins of humanity," from the "underside of history." In the North it would seem that often we may find comprehensive intellectual theological systems looking for a praxis; whereas, in the South, there is plenty of praxis, striving to find perhaps an adequate theological underpinning.

At the risk of being accused of using overworked jargon, theology has a crucial part to play in the missionary task of leading human beings from alienation to wholeness. Theology works from within the framework, given to us by God's revelation, of the reality of creation, the fall, redemption, and consummation. Human beings have been created to enjoy fellowship with God, with one another, and with creation; but they do not. Rather, they have constructed an order of violence — anger against and rejection of God's just claim on their life, brutality, disorder within human communities, and violation of the environment — in which they are always on the edge of self-destruction.

Theology begins, not just with the prophetic word, but with the incarnate Word. When it is true to itself, it will follow the movement of the Word from the heart of God (John 1:18) to the depths of the world (Eph. 4:9) and back again. As well as a prophetic role on behalf of God, it has a priestly and servant role to fulfill in behalf of wounded humanity.

The true theologian, then, cannot avoid the challenge of knowing personally life in its most traumatic forms. Again, I understand that this is a fundamental aspect of the globalization program of theological education: "crossing boundaries and discovering the realities that lie on the other side" (Lesher 1993:44). Moreover, in order to understand better the way social life develops historically, he or she will have to learn to use wisely the tools of sociopolitical and cultural analysis, though without ever making a fetish of pure methodology. Here the warning of Douglas Meeks (1993:257) is timely, though dire:

> It is true that both criticism and innovation stem from what we may call the power of suffering. But seminaries [theology] will not be changed by the mere experience of the poor and poverty. Modernity's pervasive liberalism can absorb and coopt any experience of the negative.

Together with experience and analysis must go the tough, universally valid, hope-inspiring project of the redemptive reign of God. Thus theology can help the missionary church to move from observation, feeling, and intellectual appraisal to a project of transformation only by setting out a model of what transformed human beings and communities would look like. Changed conditions of living and changed people are mutually reinforcing.

Transformation means leaving behind one form of living and working out another. In biblical terms it is the renunciation of the pattern of this age, which is under judgment and passing away (1 Cor. 2:6–8), and an entering into the pattern of the age to come, which is the eschatological fulfillment of God's righteous rule in the joy and power of the spirit of Christ.

Theology, in all its disciplines, is to be done unapologetically as a conscious handmaid to this process of renunciation, conversion, and entering into the birth pangs of a new world. It does not need, any longer, to bow to the alien criteria of the academy (it never did), for its real identity and purpose are fulfilled by being a resource in the service of God's mission to bring all things into subjection to Christ.

3

Running the Race

Theology in Christ's Way

An interesting controversy, probably symptomatic of a certain intellectual consensus in our society, broke out recently in the theological department of one of the British universities. It was alleged by a group of the students that a strong emphasis on Christian texts and a Christian interpretation of reality manifests unfair discrimination. They declared that, because they did not necessarily give any strict allegiance to the Christian faith, they did not feel properly included in the process of study that, again according to them, is their obvious right. Given that we are talking about a department that has traditionally concentrated on theological matters relating to the Christian faith, and that this is made plain to inquiring students both in the relevant prospectus and in the processes of interview, we must conclude that the students in question wanted to move the theological goal posts farther apart in the interests, presumably, of interreligious comprehension, cultural broad-mindedness, and radical noncommitment. For these reasons, and maybe others, they were not content to accept the perfectly legitimate, open stance adopted.

One may surmise that the inference to be drawn from this incident is that from now on the only legitimate way of studying theology is to allow every conceivable point of view an equal opportunity.[29] Many impartial observers would see the students' request as eminently reasonable, indeed absolutely just. So deeply ingrained in the mindset of our culture is the notion that theology belongs to a set of disciplines that do not possess any final criteria for distinguishing between conflicting opinions that it seems intolerable to start from a position of conviction and commitment.

Personally, I can only view the incident as symptomatic of a deep malaise in our Western culture: it seems to be generally assumed that we understand ourselves and our society better if we listen to as many conflicting voices as possible. In our postmodern and deconstructionist mood there is a conflict of interpretations, which much contemporary thought believes is intrinsically impossible to resolve. It is a malaise or, to use stronger and more direct language, a dangerous disease because it abandons all sensible distinctions between reality and fantasy, and therefore makes a nonsense of all normal assumptions about living.

Logically, this kind of perspective is also likely to have devastating effects on the classical view of mission. Christian mission is predicated on the apostolic nature of the church — that communities of people prepared to accept the stigma of following Jesus Christ of Nazareth, rather than any other, are sent by him into the heart of the world to carry out specific tasks in his name. The scope of mission is universal (pluralist in the sense of multiple and diverse), but the foundation is absolutely particular (and therefore incompatible with an ill considered open-mindedness): it springs from the heart and will of God uniquely and truthfully revealed in the life and mission of Jesus Christ, and it is to be carried out in Christ's way.

The pluralist (in the sense of heterogeneous but not ultimately incompatible) alternative to Christian mission assumes that any activities that cannot be shared by people of all faiths and by other people of goodwill should not be undertaken by the church. Thus, for example, it is highly commendable to work with Buddhists in Sri Lanka to end communal strife, but it is unacceptable to seek to persuade Buddhists that only salvation through Christ can deliver them from the most fundamental human predicaments that are at the root of the strife in the first place. Likewise, it is desirable for Christians to work hand in hand with people, whatever their faith commitment, to end the misery of homelessness, child abuse, violence against women, and other evils of our contemporary society; but it is an abuse of friendship, or of employment conditions, or of the cultural convention not to discuss religion in public to share with them the good news that Jesus Christ, by his spirit, *alone* has the power to restore to wholeness wounded lives of all kinds. Indeed, it is the connotation evoked by the word *alone* that causes a major scandal for all those who espouse pluralistic beliefs. It may not be used, for it is said to represent domination, discrimination, lack of respect, a belligerent, arrogant, oppressive, alienating mind-set.

The pluralistic case seems so invincible that other positions are made to look positively archaic. The reaction

of the Muslim population to Salman Rushdie's now in-
famous book *The Satanic Verses,* for example, has been
painted in the Western media as reminiscent of the worst
kind of religious intolerance as practiced in the medieval
period of Western history. Perhaps, more starkly, is the
case of liberation theology, which I have heard described
recently as premodern in its outlook, with the obvious inference that it could not be taken seriously by a society
that has "progressed" to a different consciousness about reality. This judgment is based on the insistence by liberation
theologians that there are true and false views of God,
and that a pluralistic tolerance of belief both springs from
and promotes idolatry, and idolatry always spells death for
humanity.

In a recent book (Kirk 1992), I have tried to set out the
reasons why pluralism as a conviction about belief and life,
although impossible to sustain by the use of any consistent
argument, is nevertheless dangerous because of its appeal
to inner forces beyond the reach of rational discourse (e.g.,
wistfulness, mystical intuition, enlightenment). To return
for a moment to our university students in the department
of theology, the most obvious reason why pluralism as a way
of approaching reality is dangerous is that it negates any
basis for distinguishing between beliefs and actions that are
good and those that are evil. However, in practice distinctions are drawn, for everyone believes that discrimination
is absolutely vital in certain circumstances (e.g., in the refusal to appoint pedophiles to work in children's homes or
to choose a member of a Fascist organization to operate an
antiracist program in a local council). The examples may
seem ludicrous, though in reality they have proved all too

possible; but the point at issue is that there are bound-aries that everyone recognizes. In doing so they declare that pluralism, although it may have an immediate emotional appeal, in the real world is incapable of engendering any kind of consistent practice.

In the present climate this discussion seems to me to be absolutely essential. It helps us to focus carefully on the nature, purpose, and process of Christian theology and its relation to Christian mission. In one sense it seems obvi-ous that theology cannot but have a mission: however it is taught, and for whatever purpose, it is based on a set of convictions and communicates a message. Nevertheless, the mission in question is not necessarily compatible at all with Christian mission. Indeed, as already argued, the dominant model of theology, which still undergirds most of our ap-proach to theological education in the West, is marginal to, when not distinctly hostile to, an identifiable Christian understanding of what it means to be involved in God's mission in the world.

As we have noted, theological method over the last two hundred years has been dominated by skepticism. To borrow a famous phrase of the young Karl Marx, it has proceeded on the basis that only a "ruthless critique of all things" can strip away the (assumed to be false) myths and propaganda of traditional confessional theology. Hence, the texts of Christian faith, particularly those of the Bible, have often been assumed to be guilty of the "falsification" (the creative, theological touching-up) of reality in the interests of trying to persuade others to believe a particular message. One of the most famous examples of this alleged distortion would be the supposed anti-Semitism built into the warp and woof of the apostolic preaching of Jesus (though, one might ask, to what extent can a Semite be anti-Semitic?).[30] As a line of argument, such a conclusion leaves much to be desired, for it commits the methodological error of assuming that the occasion for something to happen is also the cause of its happening.

However, there have always been problems with the historical-critical method that have perhaps only begun to be admitted in recent times. It has not been sufficiently self-critical, because it has not been aware enough of its own assumptions and biases. The "guilty-until-proved-innocent" approach has, for example, led to incredibly improbable, not to say highly bizarre, hypotheses about the history of the early church, not least in the resurrection narratives of the four Gospels. The assumption that those who believe in a uniquely true message inevitably distort history in the interests of demonstrating their case flows from a deeply skeptical approach to all knowledge; it does not necessarily reflect a critical process, sound in its procedure. Those who want to present a contrary case must, by the same token, be equally guilty of distorting history. If one accepts the major assumption of the inevitable existence of distortion, the only access to historical data that anyone could have would be through mutually incompatible historical misrepresentations. No one really believes that history is subject to such vagaries, for if one did, one would give up the task of historical investigation altogether.

A truly critical method would uncover the implicit faith commitment inherent in the stance that has moved from a genuinely healthy suspicion of others' motives and interests to a pathological skepticism in all cases. Consistent skepticism ends in nihilism, a constitutional incapacity to believe anything. Such a position, if really adhered to, would paralyze all activity. It is recognized today as a real illness of which the sufferer needs to be healed. It is also interesting to note how the alleged "masters" of suspicion (Marx, Nietzsche, and Freud), in advocating their own theories about human life and values, made many wildly uncritical assumptions and statements.

Unfortunately, in my estimation, the dominant approach to theology in the West has been rooted in skepticism, rather than in a properly self-critical critical method. This continues in some academic institutions and profoundly affects the teaching of theology as a discipline necessary to learn on the way to ministry in, or on behalf of, the Christian community. To use the word myself, I am skeptical of there being a major change in the way theology is approached in the West as an intellectual task, as long as the traditional presuppositions, which seem to control many of the university departments and which I outlined earlier, are not substantially revised. It is the burden of this study that the beginning of substantive change has to happen through an open acknowledgment that theology by its nature is missionary.[31]

The divide between the grass-roots church and the pursuit of theology, the former often seen as espousing an anti-intellectual approach to belief, will continue to grow unless and until theology is put critically at the service of the church's mission. No doubt the dominant model will continue in existence, though in the context of a growing Third World church and a shrinking Western one, it will become increasingly marginal to the whole Christian com-

munity worldwide. Its function will be largely formal —
to grant qualifications recognized by those who control
academia. As long as these are sufficiently valued, academia
will be able to sell its goods in the market. But the value
in the first place will be acceptability within the "scholarly"
community.[32]

Without doubt there have been many movements in
modern theology in the West — dialectic, existential, process, narrative, secular, dialogical, postliberal (Ford 1989) —
but none of them are movements for real change, for none
of them have challenged the modern intellectual roots of
the theological enterprise. To use a marketing metaphor,
in spite of the different wrappings and labels, they are but
different brands of the same fundamental commodity. The
only real break is happening on "the underside of history,"
where different criteria of what is critical theology (prophetic, not skeptical) and what is authentic theology (that
which promotes real liberation for a new way of being
human in community, not that which demands autonomy)
are being applied. Christian theology is being reappropriated for the liberating task of mission among the poor and
wretched of the world — all those who lack the full means
for a truly human life, whether material, emotional, or spiritual. My hope is that it may be reappropriated again in the
West from its alien and alienating existence in academia to
fulfill its true calling.

My thesis is that it is impossible to conceive of theology apart from mission. All true theology is, by definition,
missionary theology, for it has as its object the study of the
ways of a God who is by nature missionary and a foundation text written by and for missionaries. Mission as a

discipline is not, then, the roof of a building that completes the whole structure, already constructed by blocks that stand on their own, but both the foundation and the mortar in the joints, which cements together everything else. Theology should not be pursued as a set of isolated disciplines. It assumes a model of cross-cultural communication, for its subject matter both stands over against culture and relates closely to it. Therefore, it must be interdisciplinary and interactive.

In one sense, to view theology in this way is to make a virtue out of a necessity, for every conceivable way of doing theology carries its own particular message. If one studies, say, the writings of people as diverse as Don Cupitt, John Hick, Robert Schreiter, Leonardo Boff, Elsa Tamez, C. S. Song, Edward Schillebeeckx, Elisabeth Schüssler Fiorenza, Kwesi Dickson, and Lesslie Newbigin, one can discern immediately a certain missionary, or "evangelistic," intention, even when the missionary objectives are diametrically opposed.

How should we understand mission? It has become fashionable in some circles to affirm that "we do not know what mission is," or at least to be allergic to statements about mission. One reason for this is understandable: as modern business in recent years has increasingly used the terminology of mission, it behooves us to be cautious. Indeed, if mission is taken to mean a triumphalistic and crusading spirit, then we need to be extremely circumspect. However, an over-reticent attitude may be the result of confusing ends and means: mission has been judged an unfortunate word, not because of its rationale but because of the way it has often been implemented.

In my estimation it is essential to attempt a definition; otherwise implicit, unwholesome views may go unchallenged. The danger is that if we do not know what mission is, neither do we know what it is not, and that could lead us to abandon the critical task of denying certain versions of mission, which precisely bring the whole notion into disrepute. The often implied view that definition entails arrogance could be turned right round: surely the arrogance is in denying knowledge of mission, when the good news of Jesus and the kingdom is the indispensable starting point for understanding anything.

I believe that the former Commission for World Mission and Evangelism of the World Council of Churches[33] was right to emphasize that mission is appropriate only if carried out in Christ's way, because the way of Christ is the standard by which all mission is to be judged. "Mission flows from a desire to follow in the way of Jesus, who healed the sick, associated with outsiders, rebuked the self-righteous, challenged the absolute power of the state, restored people's dignity, opposed legalistic and corrupt religious practices, and ultimately gave his life to demonstrate that even enemies were encompassed in his love. Jesus tells his disciples to 'go and do likewise.'"[34]

My continuing conviction, as will by now be obvious, is that the health of the whole Christian community ultimately depends on its ability to move from dependence on the present dominant model of theology (without abandoning its input, where this has been creative) to one in which the whole theological enterprise is consciously put at the service of the call "to follow in Christ's way." Theological education, then, will be one of the major processes

by which people are helped to enter more fully into all the
dimensions of "Christ's way." This in no way implies the
abandonment of a proper critical task. However, it places
the source of criticism where, for a Christian, it must surely
belong — in the prophetic Word, which is "sharper than any
two-edged sword," not in the assumptions of a culture that,
in its formal denial of a unified truth, devours itself by its
vulnerability to every kind of weird and bizarre fantasy.

Liberating the Theological Curriculum: The Outline of a Scheme

In conclusion I would like to attempt tentatively to develop a model of theological education that breaks free from
the classical scheme of theological disciplines in order to
find an appropriate pedagogical way of fulfilling the mission of theology as outlined in these pages. My model is
based on four cardinal points of theological discipleship —
pilgrimage, message, communication, and action — which,
I believe, faithfully reflect a missionary theology done in
Christ's way.

The model contains four learning stages. The first con-
sists of an initial analysis of what the participants believe,
know, understand, and have experienced — that is, their
pilgrimage up to the point of embarking on formal theological education. At the beginning of the course of studies,
considerable time will be given to allow participants to explore their own background. They will be encouraged to
recall and reflect upon their own family life, both past and
present, their experience of education, the formation of
their values and convictions, likes and dislikes, their attitude

toward and involvement in paid work, the process by which they came to Christian faith, and their experience of the church. In this way, they will spend time looking at their individual journeys as human beings and as Christian disciples. The rationale for this first stage is quite simple; it is based on the educational principle that learning best takes place within a consciously recognized process of growth, development, change, and new horizons.

Recently I met a man about forty years old training for the ordained ministry. In talking to him it became apparent that little or nothing of his past life and experience had been taken up into the educational task he was embarked upon. Here was a person with considerable skills and experience learned in secular employment, with a young family of his own, who had spent some years as a lay leader in his church, and who had traveled overseas, being treated as if he were a tabula rasa. He was, unfortunately, being subjected to what may be called the "package" or "conveyor-belt" view of theological education. In the limited time available to him, he was required by the college and the church authorities to pass through a particular set of predetermined hoops that, if successfully negotiated, made him fit for ordination.

Another reason for starting at this place is the need, in my opinion, to treat a person's views and way of life with integrity. When I first set out on the path of theological study, it was the expressed view of one of the teaching staff — a well-known theologian on the British scene, now retired — that the beliefs of all the students were probably wrong, certainly inadequate, and definitely in need of substantial change. This kind of view has been common, I believe, among a number of theological teachers. It is most paternalistic, if not arrogant. The corollary is not, I would maintain, an indifference to simplistic belief, but the inculcation of a self-critical reflective process through which people will be exposed to other opinions and given the space and support to continue their own journeys by facing new ideas, situations, and challenges.

There are a number of ways in which this first stage might be undertaken. Within a fully modularized curriculum, it could take the form of a module (called, for example, "Personal Development/Pilgrimage") in which group seminar work and personal tutorials would constitute a standard format. The educational institution would need to ensure that, as the individual participant reflects on past experience, which in some cases could include traumatic incidents, and grapples with her or his evolving grasp of the meaning and implications of faith, there is adequate pastoral support.

Assessment would be on the basis of participants' ability, through group sharing and written work, to come to terms with their past as a point of departure for their continued learning experience. It might well take the form, in part, of mutual group evaluation. Each participant would need to achieve the objectives and fulfill the requirements of this stage before he or she could go on to the more formally theological stages of the learning cycle.

The second stage, which would be an intentional complement to the first, would consist of what might be called in broad terms "cultural and social analysis." Again, the emphasis would be on a self-learning process in which participants would be enabled to acquire the relevant tools to analyze for themselves the different facets of the culture and social system in which they were nurtured and shaped. (In this way the pilgrimage would be set against a wider background, and self-understanding broadened and deepened.)

Certainly at this stage there will be more direct input, on the assumption that authentic cultural and social analysis is quite a sophisticated procedure, requiring acquired skills and knowledge in the fields of anthropology and sociology. At the same time, participants would be encouraged to observe and interpret aspects of culture for themselves, being engaged perhaps in a limited way in their own survey of trends. Here the method of compiling and presenting portfolios of material would form a useful way of combining personal observation of live situations with the study of theoretical material in the relevant social disciplines. In an educational process built on the triad "see, judge, act," these two stages would correspond to "see."

The third stage focuses upon "judge," or, in the four-point model, on "message" and "communication." (The methodological assumption is that judgment is dependent upon both a given perspective and a process of interaction between personal reflection, observation, analysis, and faith conviction.) It begins quite deliberately with a survey of the sources of Christian faith. Because we are talking about theological education for mission, it will be vital to spend time exploring first the biblical foundations for mission in the way of Christ.

At this point, priority should be given to a general survey or overview of the meaning of mission in a total biblical perspective. Certainly, this would not exclude looking at the diversity of stances within the Scriptures, but diversity should not necessarily be given a privileged place, as if it were self-evident that the unity of the biblical message was more questionable than its plurality. Of course, many ways of approaching the text of Scripture will be used, not least in order to immerse oneself in the original context and to listen to the understandings coming from Christians in Africa, Asia, and Latin America.

This way of proceeding will probably require a considerable adjustment of traditional ways of teaching the Old and New Testaments. What will change most fundamentally are the aims and objectives of the course(s). Knowledge of the text, its initial historical context and its original purpose, intention, or function, will be combined with an appreciation of its missiological implications at the time of writing, during subsequent canonical history, and for present times. Such a process may be divided into two or three different modules. The input would be mainly in the form of giving participants tools for doing their own exploration and then guiding and facilitating their work in a continuing process of feedback.

This stage in the educational sequence would also include selected historical surveys and the comparison, across both time and space, of different theological stances regarding Christian mission. In the first instance, it might be appropriate to concentrate on ecclesiological concerns, with a view to identifying the variety of missiological assumptions that are implied by the different types of church organization and activity. This way of doing theology picks up the insistence of liberation thinking that a fundamental task of theology is to reflect critically on the praxis of the church in the light of the Word, the premise being that one has the surest guide to what the Christian community believes if one knows how it acts.

The communication component of this stage is crucial. It might even be considered a separate stage, as long as it is always closely related to what precedes it. In one sense it is part of the process by which the authenticity of mission is tested. It is interactive in that the three stages of study undertaken so far — personal pilgrimage, cultural/ social analysis, and missionary message — are allowed to intersect in a creative hermeneutical procedure. Here time would be given to exploring how Christian faith has made an impact on culture, and vice versa, and to looking at ethical questions at both the micro and macro levels, but always, as a first task, trying to relate the issues to the participants' own comprehension of life and faith.

It would probably make sense, after spending some time on the third stage, to encourage the participants to bring their own questions of communication — of relating the message to situations and hearers — to the discussion, so that a continuing agenda, at least in part, may be set by them.

The fourth and final stage is action. Pastoral practice, counseling, evangelism, community development, and other types of involvement in the community, youth work, education, and worship would be included within the scope of this section. The method would require reflection arising out of the actual work undertaken, on the premise that the process — "see, judge, act" — continually repeats itself. This circle also has its own internal logic in the sense that involvement in the community (e.g., in the rehabilitation of drug addicts or mental health care), demands an informed understanding of current theory and practice in these fields.[35]

One could presume with some confidence that, if the model of learning advocated here were carried out with some degree of success, fresh questions for Christian mission would be arising out of both the biblical and historical studies and the opportunities for practical involvement. It would, therefore, be a crucial part of every stage that both individuals and small work teams would accompany their studies and practical exposures with their own continual assessment, perhaps in the form of a journal. This would concentrate on the areas where further clarification of the message, the missionary task of the church, the social and cultural reality in which the participant is immersed, and ethical questions are needed.

There is no particular time sequence suggested for this model of theological education. However, as the process is in its essence spiral, it can be stretched or compressed into whatever time is available. If one assumes that participants are engaged in full-time study within a modular system based on semesters, then the first year of study might include the following components:

First semester: Personal Development, Cultural Analysis, Social Analysis, Biblical Foundation for Mission (I).

Second semester: Biblical Foundation for Mission (II), Historical Models of Mission, Disciplines of Care, Introduction to Ethical Thought.

Each year, or discrete part of the educational sequence, should end with every participant writing a full, critical account of her or his own learning process, including a range of topics that need to be picked up and further developed for the next year or subsequent sequence. This study would comprise one third of the year's work for the purposes of assessment and qualification.

Clearly, the method that I am outlining and the rationale on which it is based rest on establishing a particular kind of relationship between educator and educated. It will require less formal input on the part of the staff team and more time given to supervision and feedback. The educator will be more a resource person than a conveyor of knowledge in the classroom. It is also immediately obvious that the traditional schema of theological training has been largely abandoned. In its place there is a model that calls upon the resources of the biblical, historical, systematic, ethical, and pastoral disciplines, but in new combinations that reflect a different overall objective. There is a sense in which the model requires a new mind-set: mission is not a separate subject, but an all-pervasive dimension that orients the purpose, content, approach, and method of assessment of each module taken.

At later points in the program, interdisciplinary seminars on particular topics related to the church's mission may become a major feature of the process. One example of this might be the role of the church in peace making. This would require, naturally, biblical and systematic reflection on the nature and causes of violence and the meaning of reconciliation and peace. It would involve a study of the religious dimensions of both past and present conflicts. Observation of actual situations of conflict resolution and the analysis of other case studies would also be vital components of such a seminar. It might last long enough to be able to trace discernible changes in a particular situation, thus helping the participants to learn lessons as a process was unfolding.

There will be different ways of putting this model into effect. Part of its attractiveness, in my opinion, is its flexibility in being able to make time for issues that arise in the course of the process. Thus, neither participant nor course director will necessarily know what the agenda of study may be six to twelve months ahead. What I have been trying to describe is a pattern of learning that consciously operates within four major points of reference: the Christian message, the participant's own pilgrimage, the life and witness of the Christian community, and the society in which she or he will be called to mission in Christ's way. It is intended to create an appropriate educational response to the principles and proposals outlined in the first two parts of this study, namely, that authentic theology at the end of the second millennium can only be theology "for the sake of mission."

Notes

1. I take the word "reinvent" from the subtitle of Leonardo Boff's celebrated book *Ecclesiogenesis: The Base Communities Reinvent the Church* (1986) because of its evocative sense of an exciting new project.

2. I use the term "South" in preference to either "Third World" or "Two-Thirds World" to denote all parts of the world that, from the fifteenth century onward, became the object of the European (and later the North American) aspiration to conquer new territories and new markets.

3. David Kelsey (1993) elaborates this ideal model at some length under the nomenclature of "Berlin:" "The overarching and organizing goal of the university was to be research and teaching students how to do research; its goal was to be inquiry that aims to master the truth about whatever subject is studied" (:13).

4. The definition given by the *Concise Oxford Dictionary* of the word "academic" is quite instructive: "1. scholarly. 2. abstract, unpractical, theoretical, cold, merely logical."

5. This was in connection with a lay training institute, known originally as the London Institute for Contemporary Christianity and now called Christian Impact.

6. Bosch (1991:489–90) gives an excellent summary of the various interpretations of the meaning of theology.

7. I fully recognize the inadequacy of attempting to set down any one description of theology on paper; sometimes the most interesting insights into the various ways of doing theology come through

an analysis of what is done in practice! My own statement is not a refined definition. It is intended, rather, as a working model.

8. The "compare and contrast" kind of question so beloved by examiners.

9. The same can be said for certain other texts that make similar claims as to their origin, similar demands upon the reader, and a similar impact in concrete historical situations — most notably the Qur'an.

10. It is, perhaps, one of the consequences of the current tendency to treat all cultures as relative and conditional that the separation between rationalistic cultures and "wisdom" cultures has become a commonplace.

11. Of course, the scientific method is portrayed as an ideal procedure. In reality, social and personal circumstances intervene to make the processes less straightforward, sometimes causing theories to be held for a long time against what seems to be the prevailing evidence. Nevertheless, scientific work would not proceed if the ideal did not remain in place.

12. Since approximately the 1960s, theologians have begun to discover the importance of the social science disciplines to aspects of their work. This has led, in some cases, to a certain naïveté about their efficaciousness. Thus, Wood maintains that theological inquiry is made rigorously critical by incorporating the relevant "secular" disciplines of history, philosophy, or the human sciences (Kelsey 1993:206). The truth is that all these disciplines may also be impregnated by ideological presumptions that require just as much disentangling. They cannot, therefore, be used as value-free tools to judge the ideological commitment of theological inquiry.

13. However, much more sophisticated ways of understanding God's interaction with the world are opened up by the new physics (Barbour 1990: chap. 4.I).

14. The assertion that any claims to events being caused other than by phenomena in principle measurable and testable have to be disqualified from rational inquiry.

15.   O my white-burdened Europe, across so many maps greed
        zigzags. One voice and the nightmare of a dominant chord:

> defences, self-mirroring, echoings, myriad overtones of
> shame. Never again one voice. Out of malaise, out of need
> our vision cries (O'Siadhail 1992).

16. Though the historical context in which it has arisen may
be different, the approach has much in common with the romantic strain of modern thought since the Enlightenment, which
came to its denouement in existentialism (Mitchell 1980:chaps. 1
and 3).

17. "One might say generally that modern liberal theology is that
kind of theology that speaks of God under the conditions laid down
by the theory of natural liberty and the laws of the market" (Meeks
1993:249).

18. "In the social sphere evil occurs when a group's self-
absolutizing of its particularity violently utilizes other groups."
The notion of the equal validity of the many voices cuts away
the grounds for censuring "the absolutizing of particularity" (Meeks
1993:257).

19. For an account of the subject matter of the thesis, see Walter Riggans (1992:130–32), "Messianic Judaism: A Case of Identity
Denied."

20. The last section of this study will develop this kind of process
and will suggest an alternative model for the theological curriculum
that will have mission at its center.

21. I have tried to explore some of the major aspects of its impact
upon the whole theological scene in a monograph (Kirk 1983).

22. "Robert Heilbroner says that the nature of our society is ac-
cumulation of wealth as power, and that the logic of our society is
exchange of commodities" (Meeks 1993:250).

23. If, on the basis of historical hindsight, it is legitimate to draw
a fairly clear distinction between the abiding apostolic gospel and the
doctrinal and practical accretions often promoted by the church, and
generally accepted in society as a whole, it is probably true to say
that there never was such a time.

24. In an unpublished paper given to a group of missiologists in
Paris, January 1992.

25. Lamin Sanneh (1993) elaborates and criticizes the princi-

ple of territoriality, deeply embedded in the European Christian heritage.

26. In a recent piece of research (Kirk forthcoming), I have myself explored the nature, extent, and consequences of modern concepts and experiences of freedom in secular societies.

27. The example that has come to mind recently is that of the American indigenous cultures, largely liquidated through the expansion of the European powers, beginning five hundred years ago. The denial of full human equality to those vanquished militarily was without excuse. However, to lay a justified blame on the attitudes and actions of the conquistadores is not to be confused with a certain modern tendency to view the pre-Columbian cultures through romantic, rose-tinted spectacles. Some of them were also mightily oppressive and vicious with regard to minorities.

28. See particularly the essays by Jane Smith (:90–103) and Robert Schreiter (:122–33) in Evans, Evans, and Roozen (1993).

29. In the realm of interreligious study, this should mean not only the beliefs and stances of the major world religions, primal or traditional religions, and popular versions of all of these, but also every esoteric and colorful set of beliefs and practices that might come under the collective heading of "new religious movements." The fact that rarely is Christianity, Islam, Mormonism, Scientology, or Hare Krishna (vary the selection, as you like) treated with the same respect and depth of consideration demonstrates that most pluralists are likely to be quite discriminatory about their dialogical dedication.

30. In all fairness, if the message of the early (Jewish) Christians was an interpretation of Jewish history and theological tradition, albeit disputed, then refusal to believe it was, according to the terms of the argument, equally anti-Semitic. To deduce anti-Semitism from the pages of the New Testament is, of course, a historical anachronism.

31. David Bosch (1991:494) states that theology ceases to be theology (per se) if it loses its missionary character. If one accepts his thesis that missiology's task is to highlight theology's reference to the world, one might then dispense altogether with a separate subject

called missiology. In other words, missiology = missionary theology = all authentic (done in a missionary spirit and context) theology.

32. Kosuke Koyama reflects on the historical and cultural aberration of the so-called scientific method. "Why," he asks, "has theological education paid more attention to the 'scientific nature of theological truths' than to the messages of the First Commandment and of the Sacrament of the Holy Eucharist? Was it because Western theologians wanted to be accepted by the post-Enlightenment university?" He also criticizes professional, academic theology for its distance from vernacular language, pointing out that, although "it has become rather common among Western theologians to speak of the 'Strange World of the Bible,' in many cultures, the world of the Bible may not seem so strange" (Koyama 1993:91, 93). Even in the West the strangeness of the Bible is a general assumption brought to the study of theology, not a conclusion derived from it.

33. Now insipidly called Unit II: Education, Communication and Witness. The phrase "Mission in the Way of Christ" was the theme of the 1989 San Antonio conference of the Commission.

34. From the *Mission Affirmation* of the Selly Oak Colleges' School of Mission and World Christianity (1992).

35. The kind of possibilities that can be explored and how they fit into a new paradigm of theological education have been set out in a series of essays that describe the experience of theological institutions in Chicago and elsewhere (Thistlethwaite and Cairns 1994)

References Cited

Barbour, Ian. 1990. *Religion in an Age of Science.* London: SCM Press.

Bloom, Allan. 1987. *The Closing of the American Mind.* Harmondsworth, Eng.: Penguin.

Boff, Leonardo. 1986. *Ecclesiogenesis: The Base Communities Reinvent the Church.* Maryknoll, N.Y.: Orbis Books.

Bosch, David J. 1991. *Transforming Mission.* Maryknoll, N.Y.: Orbis Books.

Costas, Orlando E. 1986. "Theological Education and Mission," in C. Rene Padilla, ed., *New Alternatives in Theological Education.* Oxford: Regnum Books.

Evans, Alice F., Robert Evans, and David A. Roozen. 1993. *The Globalization of Theological Education.* Maryknoll, N.Y.: Orbis Books.

Ford, David, ed. 1989. *The Modern Theologians: An Introduction to Christian Theology in the Twentieth Century.* Vols. 1 and 2. Oxford: Blackwell.

Hebblethwaite, Margaret. 1994. *Base Communities: An Introduction.* Mahwah, N.J.: Paulist Press.

Ives, Eric. 1992. "The Gospel and History," in Hugh Montefiore, ed., *The Gospel and Contemporary Culture.* London: Mowbray.

Kelsey, David. 1993. *Between Athens and Berlin: The Theological Education Debate.* Grand Rapids: Eerdmans.

Kirk, J. Andrew. 1983. *Theology and the Third World Church.* Downers Grove, Ill.: InterVarsity Press.

————. 1986. "Liberation Theology and Local Theologies," in Anthony Harvey, ed., *Theology in the City*. London: SPCK.

————. 1992. *Loosing the Chains: Religion as Opium and Liberation*. London: Hodder & Stoughton.

————. Forthcoming. *The Meaning of Freedom: A Study of Secular, Muslim, and Christian Views*.

Koyama, Kosuke. 1993. "Theological Education: Its Unities and Diversities." *Theological Education* 30, Supplement I (Autumn).

Kritzinger, J. N. J., and W. A. Saayman, eds. 1990. *Mission in Creative Tension: A Dialogue with David Bosch*. Pretoria: South African Missiological Society.

Lesher, William. 1993. "Meanings of Globalization: Living the Faith Under the Conditions of the Modern World," in Alice F. Evans et al. Pp. 33–50.

Link, Hans-Georg, ed. 1987. *Apostolic Faith Today*. Geneva: World Council of Churches.

The Listener. November 5, 12, 19, 1970. "Theology, Drugs and Zen." London: British Broadcasting Corp.

Meeks, M. Douglas. 1993. "Global Economy and the Globalization of Theological Education," in Alice F. Evans et al. Pp. 247–261.

Milbank, John. 1990. *Theology and Social Theory: Beyond Secular Reason*. Oxford: Blackwell.

Mitchell, Basil. 1980. *Morality: Religious and Secular*. Oxford: Clarendon Press.

Munoz, Ronaldo. 1991. *The God of Christians*. Maryknoll, N.Y.: Orbis Books.

Newbigin, Lesslie. 1990. *The Gospel in a Pluralist Society*. London: SPCK.

————. 1991. *Truth to Tell: The Gospel as Public Truth*. London: SPCK.

O'Siadhail, Michael. 1992. *Hail! Madam Jazz*. Chester Springs, Pa.: Dufour Editions.

Polanyi, Michael. 1958. *Personal Knowledge: Towards a Post-Critical Philosophy*. London: Routledge & Kegan Paul.

Riggans, Walter. 1992. "Messianic Judaism: A Case of Identity De-
    nied." *International Bulletin of Missionary Research* 16:3 (July).

Sanneh, Lamin. 1993. *Encountering the West. Christianity and the
    Global Cultural Process: The African Dimension.* London: Mar-
    shall Pickering.

Schreiter, Robert J. 1985. *Constructing Local Theologies.* London:
    SCM Press.

———. 1993. "Globalization as Cross-Cultural Dialogue," in Al-
    ice F. Evans et al. Pp. 122–133.

Selly Oak Colleges, School of Mission and World Christianity.
    1992. *Mission Affirmation.* Birmingham: Selly Oak Colleges.

Shaull, Richard. 1991. *The Reformation and Liberation Theology:
    Insights for the Challenges of Today.* Louisville: Westminster/
    John Knox.

Smith, Jane. 1993. "Globalization as Ecumenical/Interfaith Dia-
    logue," in Alice F. Evans et al. Pp. 90–103.

Thistlethwaite, Susan, and George Cairns. 1994. *Beyond Theologi-
    cal Tourism: Mentoring as a Grassroots Approach to Theological
    Education.* Maryknoll, N.Y.: Orbis Books.

Wood, Charles. 1985. *Vision and Discernment.* Atlanta: Scholars
    Press.

Yu, Carver T. 1987. *Being and Relation: A Theological Critique
    of Western Dualism and Individualism.* Edinburgh: Scottish
    Academic Press.